For Michel

Learn to think like a scrapyard worker, a visual magnet, a mental chameleon, Madonna and Ali G in one body, your little cousin, and a fish on a mountain

Left Brain

Right Brain

Learn about the design process and develop ideas for all design disciplines.

Understanding design

For designers, educators, students, and others
This book is for anyone who would like to learn and understand design in more detail and more deeply. What is design? What is creativity? And what mentality and conditions are needed to guarantee a productive design process? How can someone hone their work as a designer or come to appreciate design itself? What about those who work with designers in a team or as clients or commissioners?

The ideas in this book are relevant for design in its broadest sense, such as creating artifacts, experiences, and transformations through communication design, product design, interaction design, architecture design, fashion design, interior design, advertising, brand design, photography, and more.

Left Brain
The first part of the book is mostly an analysis of the design process. It explains what design is, how to organise its process, what mindset is needed to handle it, and what conditions are instrumental in achieving success.

Right Brain
The second part is about generating more and better ideas. Its contents are more visual and focussed on stimulating the imagination. It describes powerful methods that boost creativity and visual ideation—abilities that can be learned, developed, and applied even beyond the context of design.

If you are more interested in learning how to create better ideas, you can jump directly to Part 2 of this book, page 60.

Part 1

Left Brain

- What is design?
- Creating value
- Design and beauty
- Starting design projects
- Design mentality
- Conditions and habits that help design
- Good design process
- Reversed ideating

Design is about communication, identification, function, and construction.

Bring a message or tell a story.
(Advertising & Communication Design)

Communication

10

5

Create space and
three-dimensionality.
(Architecture & Interior Design)

Add personality and
recognition.
(Branding & Identity Design)

Construction ●●●●●●●●●●●● **Design** ●●●●●●●●●●● **Identification**

10   5   5   10

5

10

Function

Improve usability and navigation.
(Product & Interface Design)

What is design?

Design is a process begun by thoroughly understanding a topic by doing research, then coming up with original ideas and solutions that have value and are relevant based on that research. The ideas part can start with a sketch or a visual to show the appearance, personality, and function of a space, an object, or message before it is built, made, or communicated.

Four purposes

Design has four objectives: communication, identification, function, and construction. Communication means information design and advertising, with a focus on delivering a message or telling a story. Identification means branding and identity design, through which personality is added to organisations, products, services, and places. Coming up with functional solutions, and designing practical tools, or guiding users with clear steps through a physical or digital space, as in product and interface design is the third objective. And construction, meaning interior design and architecture—creating three-dimensional experiences—is the final objective.

Often design solutions satisfy each of the four design purposes. They can be used to define ambitions during the design process or to evaluate designs after they are made.

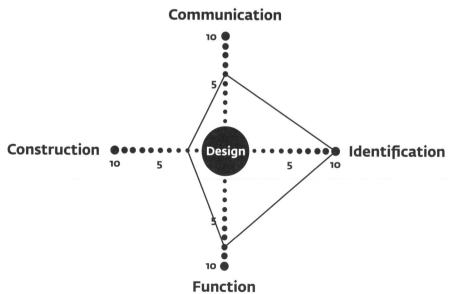

Communication

Construction

Design

Identification

Function

• *Striping Dutch national police. Studio Dumbar – Gert Dumbar and Joost Roozekrans. Photography, Lex van Pieterson. 1991.*

The striping was designed to satisfy multiple purposes in the simplest way. One set of fluorescent orange and reflective blue diagonal stickers, two logos, and a simple instruction can transform any white car model into a police car. The striping informs everyone, 'This is the police.' The design is also functional: it makes the car visible day and night and allows the car to be used as a roadblock. This design accomplishes quite a bit through communication, but hardly involves any construction.

Design can create value—economic value, but also social and environmental value.

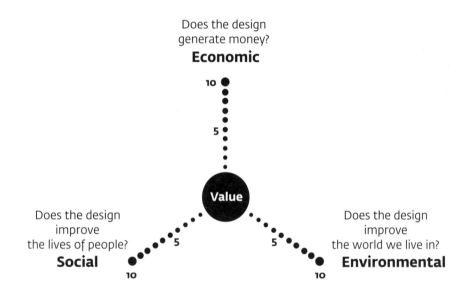

Does the design
generate money?
Economic

10

5

Value

Does the design
improve
the lives of people?
Social

5

10

Does the design
improve
the world we live in?
Environmental

5

10

Creating value

Beyond economics

Design can create value. It can make or improve a product, service, or place, and give those things meaning, purpose, and relevance. Value is often seen in economic terms, but there are more ways to create value with design. Design can also create social value by improving the conditions for how people live and connect.

More importantly, design can also create environmental value with ideas that help to improve the world we live in now, and by taking responsibility in making the world a better and more durable place for the next generations to come — not just improving the human condition, but also that of all other living organisms: plants, insects, animals…the entire ecosystem.

Precious Plastic—an open-source plastic recycling project with an active global community.

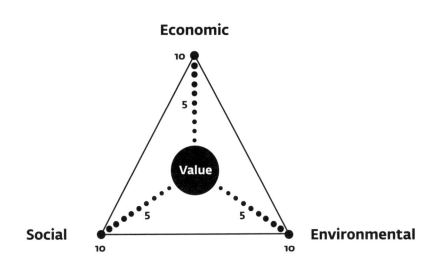

• Precious Plastic is an open-source hardware plastic recycling project. The project was started in 2013 by Dutch designer Dave Hakkens and evolves continuously. It relies on a series of machines and tools that grind, melt, and inject recycled plastic, allowing for the creation of new products out of recycled plastic on a small scale. The project allows people from around the world to set up their own small recycling company. It has an active community with more than 40,000 people involved in over 400 workspaces, either in remote sites or on-site in the Netherlands. Precious Plastic creates economic, social, and environmental value.

Designers are not just beautifiers.

Beauty is personal, culturally defined, and changes over time.

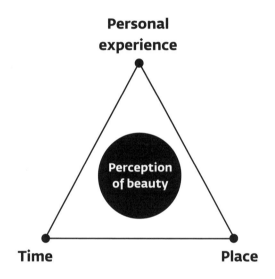

Design and beauty

Relevant design

Designers are not just beautifiers. Thinking so is a superficial way of looking at design. Everyone has a sense of beauty, but talking about beauty as a designer with clients is often tricky for the simple reason that it is so personal and subjective. It is more constructive to talk about design in terms of how well it matches with the essence of the product, the service or strategy, how well it connects with the target audience, how relevant it is, and distinctive compared with the competition.

What is beauty?

Beauty can be seen as harmony, balanced proportions, an essence. Some say it is about passion or love. Everyone has a sense of beauty, although it is not always easy to analyse what it is and how to put it into words correctly. There are a few essential things to know about beauty:

• Beauty is about personal aesthetic preferences—an individual sensation. Do not presume that others are experiencing the same sense of beauty as you are.

• Beauty is culturally defined. It is very much defined by the place in the world where you grew up, lived, and developed yourself. Things that were internalised in our youth have become part of how we see the world. When working on a design project that has to be effective in different cultures, it is essential to understand those differences.

• Beauty changes over time. What we see as beautiful today can be perceived differently in the future and may have been considered ugly in the past. Women with fair skin were the beauty standard in 18th century Europe, and still are in Asia. In Europe, though, a woman having a suntan is seen as beautiful.

Design for a client, or initiate projects yourself.

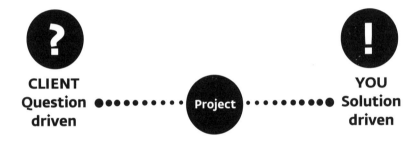

CLIENT
Question
driven

Project

YOU
Solution
driven

Starting design projects

Two ways

Roughly, there are two ways to start a design project. One is not better than the other. Both ways ultimately require excellent research skills to clearly formulate a design brief, as well as idea making and crafting skills to come up with great results.

Work for a client

The first way to start a project is to work for a client, a person or organisation that hires a designer to help to define or solve a design problem. Generally, the reward model is an agreement to start with and payment in phases during the project or once finalised.

Start projects yourself

The second approach to a project is to initiate it yourself. Problems you see a need to solve can be financed with savings, by crowd-funding, finding investors, or by making a profit from sales, subscriptions, memberships, tickets, or royalties once the project is realised.

The online marketplace and lodging broker Airbnb, offering and arranging rooms and apartments around the world, is an excellent example of a self-initiated project started by designers. But there are many more.

Projects can start with clients, commissioners, or by designers themselves; in every case, they can generate social and environmental value in addition to economic value.

Curiosity is the eagerness to learn and to being open to the new, the unknown.

. Travel and see new cultures.

. Connect with different people.

. Leave your comfort zone.

. Do not judge too fast.

Design mentality

Thinking and doing

Design is a mix of doing and thinking. The mental part, in addition to the practical part, is important. It takes the right mindset to start and to create distinct and meaningful solutions. Below are a few conditions that help develop a productive and creative design mentality.

Curiosity

Being curious is being open-minded and perceptive, having the eagerness to learn and being open to the new, the unknown. Young people are often more curious. That is because of the simple fact that most of our first-time experiences happen during the first twenty years of our lives. And first-time experiences can make everlasting, lifelong impressions. The question is, how does one stay curious and open-minded? There are a few conditions that can help curiosity:

• Travel and see new cultures. Or live in another culture.
• Meet, work, and live with people who have different ideas and backgrounds.
• Leave your comfort zone. Do things that feel challenging, new, or unusual. Doing so creates new insights and enriches your life.
• And finally, do not judge too fast. Just undergo new situations, experience them, and wait on forming an opinion until later.

Understand the impressions, feelings, and responses of others.

Believe in change for the better!

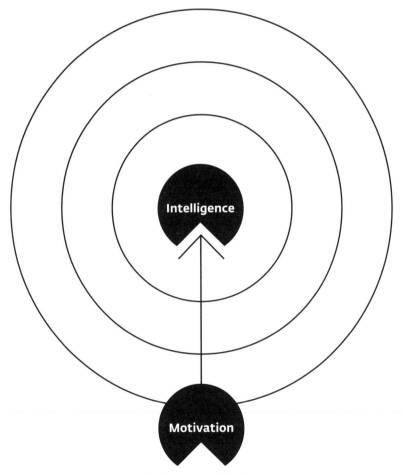

Intelligence

Motivation

Brains are not static.
You can train them
to work differently and develop.

Empathy

Empathy is focused on people. It is the ability to understand the feelings, responses, and impressions of others. Because designers solve problems for people, it is essential to know their needs and to find appropriate answers. Therefore, it is wise to test designs in advance to predict how people will react when they use a product, see a message or interface, or interact with a space.

Positivity

Positivity is the belief that things can change for the better—that design can have a positive impact on people and the world. A can-do mentality is immensely crucial if you want to get things done well. Struggling—not immediately achieving good or useful solutions—is part of producing meaningful ideas and designs. Being positive is about zest, endurance, and perseverance, not about intelligence. It is vital not to give up!

Intelligence

And now we are talking about intelligence. Intelligence is partly a matter of mentality, as it is not fixed or a given condition. The human brain is flexible, like a muscle; it can be trained and developed throughout all stages of life.

If you believe that your intelligence cannot develop and improve, you are limiting your personal growth. It is like biking while applying the hand-brake at the same time.

Being eager, having zest, and never giving up drives great design.

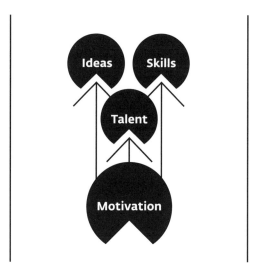

Motivation is key

Being effective in design and generating better ideas requires balancing four elementary assets:

• Ideas—coming up with relevant and valuable solutions for given problems.
• Skills—being a good craftsperson; knowing how to make things in the best possible way, manual or digital.
• Talent—doing what comes naturally, engaging in the things you find easy to do and that bring you joy while doing them.
• Motivation—having the eagerness, zest, and drive to not give up but to keep going, and with determination.

Motivation is the most important of these forces. Without motivation, design does not work. Without motivation, even the biggest talent gets wasted.

Mistakes are a good, essential, and inclusive part of every design process.

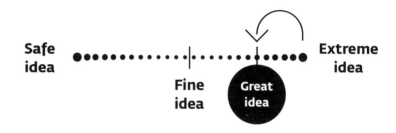

Mistakes and experiment

Making mistakes is good! Mistakes are part of every design process. It's a part of investigating new possibilities. Not having gone too far means you have not explored well enough the boundary between what works and what doesn't. It can be more effective to start with an extreme idea. You can always decide to take one or two steps back later to make the radical idea both work and be fascinating at the same time. In other words, this is the short track to a great idea. Going too far and pulling back works faster and is more effective than making small steps to develop a safe idea. Give it a try!

No embarrassment

Vulnerability is only possible after overcoming embarrassment. As children, we are very good at just giving new things a shot, trying out and experimenting without feeling any pressure or judgment by others. As grown-ups, we have unlearned how to do this. Being too aware of what others might think of us limits our exploration and our finding of new and surprising solutions. It is an active decision to let go, to allow ourselves mental freedom, and to learn how to do it. Trying to find this ability again might take some time, but is it very much worth the effort.

An essential condition for mistakes and vulnerability is to create a safe environment that encourages experimentation and allows people to be spontaneous. Celebrate trial and error.

Critical thinking always starts with asking the right questions.

Critical thinking

Critical thinking is a mentality that needs confidence. It means that you can think independently and form an opinion of your own that might differ from general assumptions or even from the opinions of authorities. It requires knowledge, logic, an investigative mind, and guts. Find out what the source of the information is and what commercial or ideological interests it might have. Actively organise forces that will challenge your findings so that you may better shape—or even reject—them.

Critical thinking is a constructive attitude. Its purpose is to sharpen presumptions and improve ideas. It is different from sarcasm; that might appear to be critical thinking, but it does not have a positive intention.

Critical thinking starts with learning to ask the right questions. It all depends on the topic, but generally, it includes a lot of 'what?', 'what not?', 'why?', and 'why not?' questions. Listening is equally essential, as is being open to alternative ideas and sharing opinions and insights with others to test and improve them.

A lot is to be learned from team members if you are willing to share and listen.

Conditions and habits that help design

Communication and collaboration

Although a single person can be creative, a team can be a powerful force to increase the speed and quality of creative output. Open communication is an essential condition to make it work. It means that team members formulate ideas in a clear, understandable way and do not speak too fast, and listeners do this with focus and attention.

Communication is also body language, making eye contact while speaking, using the face and hands to express messages, and having an open and active posture.

The atmosphere has to be one where all participants feel comfortable and at ease to speak their minds freely. Where contributions are respected, contributors get credit and there is no blaming culture. Generally, this works best if there is little or no hierarchy in the group and if egos are kept in control.

Diverse teams can generate many and diverse perspectives.

Instant visuals are the best way to test ideas.

Diversity and connectivity

Creativity blooms where different worlds come together, when people with different professions or specialisations are included. Look for diversity of cultures, genders, professions, ages, interests, and backgrounds. Diverse teams make ideas better simply because they can look at a problem from many different angles. It requires members of a diverse team to be open and adaptable. People with both a strong specialisation and a broad general interest will make teams perform better.

Connectivity helps diversity. We can use digital media to speak with individuals and groups everywhere in the world. The fact that we can use video calls, exchange files, and share ideas has provided a whole new dimension to how we work and can have effective connections.

Quick visuals

While making ideas, it is essential to make them visible quickly for two different reasons:
• First, because it is the best way to test if what you were thinking actually works or not.
• Second, to communicate ideas to the team you collaborate with, or to your client.

Visualising is testing. It is a reality check—a way to see what's working or what is missing. It is not necessary to be an expert at drawing, but if you are, it will be a great benefit to test ideas. If drawing is not your forte, there are many other ways to visualise: cutting and pasting images or existing visuals or making quick three-dimensional models from cardboard or clay. Shoot test movies to test ideas in motion. Role-play if the idea to be tested is about an interaction, an imagined service, or experience. Anything goes as long it is visual and fast.

Keep sketches to compare steps, to combine, or to continue with when new insights pop up.

Keep all sketches

Testing ideas by making them visual is essential. Once an idea is created—a process called ideation—it can be modified and optimised. This last part of fine-tuning ideas is called iteration. Sketches can be made in all kinds of media or techniques. But whatever method you use, it is vital to keep a record of all steps made. And keep them together. Editing out mistakes or overwriting stupidities, half-finished, or unfinished ideas is a no go. Everything needs to be preserved and recorded. And here is why:

• You have to be able to compare the newly-made sketch with the ones made before, to see if the changes are improvements or not—something you can only do if you have kept the earlier versions.

• The second reason is that unfinished or even once stupid ideas can prove to be useful at a later stage in the process. Or they can be constructively combined with parts of other, newer ideas.

The snake

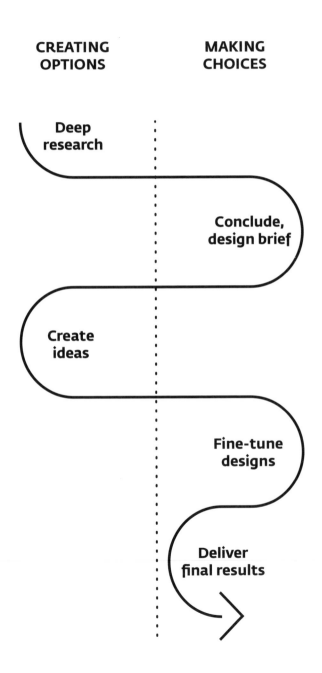

CREATING
OPTIONS

MAKING
CHOICES

Deep
research

Conclude,
design brief

Create
ideas

Fine-tune
designs

Deliver
final results

Good design process

Creating options, making choices

This part is about the design process. The snake explains this process of design and creativity visually. It is divided into two parts, two ways of thinking: The left side is about creating possibilities, the right is about making choices. This process needs a flexible mind. It demands two entirely different ways of thinking that should not happen at the same time, and have to be done with full dedication.

It starts with in-depth research—a critical and investigative part of the process—followed by selecting and prioritising knowledge. The result should be a clear and inspirational design brief. Only with a brief to refer to, can ideas be developed. Generate as many ideas as possible, with a minimum of three. Then, you can select the strongest ideas, design, fine-tune, and deliver them.

It's not a lucky shot

A good design solution is hardly ever a lucky shot, but more likely the result of a thorough design process. Knowing the process gives you a foundation and structure to optimise results. Just following the steps is not enough, of course. It needs passion and full dedication to find good and diverse content and create high-quality output.

Design without research is like taking a taxi and only saying, 'Go!'

. *Only use sources with authority.*

. *Verify significant findings.*

. *Ask, does the source have a hidden interest?*

1 • Research

What is research?

Research is an essential first step in being able to define the design problem. Collecting high-quality information from various sources allows the designer to create with an in-depth understanding of the topic itself and its associated fields.

How do you research?

There are a few essential conditions that help a designer accumulate knowledge while researching:

• Only look for sources with authority, credibility, and authenticity. There is an overload of information to be found in the age of connectivity. We can access and find information everywhere. It is vital to select information that is of high quality, meaning finding out if the source of information—the person or institution—has a specialist's knowledge or expertise.

• Check if significant findings can be verified. Information that appears to be useful and that comes from a source with authority needs to be verified by other sources.

• Find out not only who the source of information is, but also try to detect if the source has a particular interest in publishing the information offered. It can be a commercial interest, or an ideological or political interest. Knowing the sender or source is another way to check how reliable the information is.

Use many different sources, like a journalist.

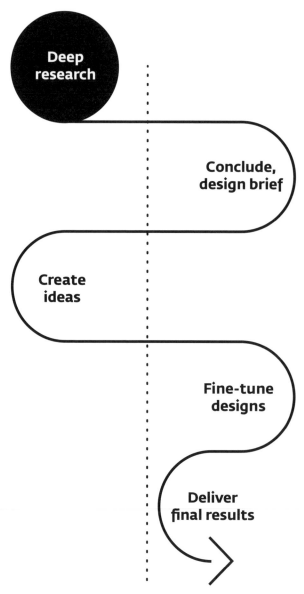

Deep research

Conclude, design brief

Create ideas

Fine-tune designs

Deliver final results

Sources

Using different types of sources helps to make research diverse. Depending on the kind of topic, the mix of sources can vary. Generally, information collected divides into qualitative and quantitative data. Qualitative information is high-value information that comes from sources with proven authority. Quantitative information is about numbers. Of course, it is vital that this data comes from reliable sources.

Possible sources to use while in the research stage:
• Online sources: written, visual, and moving image
• Articles, publications, books, and libraries
• Talks, documentaries, and movies
• Live interviews and surveys, or online surveys with target groups, stakeholders, or potential users
• Conversations with specialists
• Investigations and visits to relevant places and locations

What's the research attitude?
• Role models: journalists and scientists
• Mindset: eager and curious

Conclude and prioritise the essence, with the mindset of a judge.

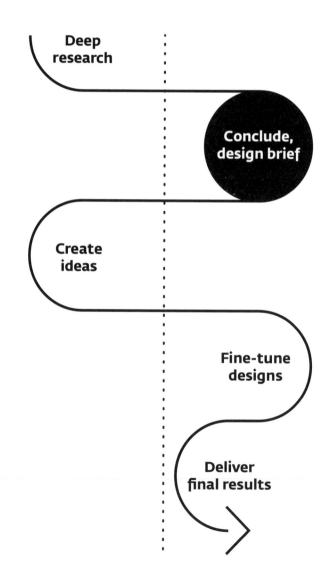

Deep research

Conclude, design brief

Create ideas

Fine-tune designs

Deliver final results

2 · Select findings

What is selecting findings?

The second step in the design process is to select and prioritize the collected findings, to draw conclusions and define the essence of the information. Why is it relevant to map how topics are connected and related? A substantial part of the collected material can become, and often is, easily ignored because some insights are quickly designated as being less relevant. But it is necessary to review, evaluate, and select all material in order to ensure that the best findings drive the process, and that no sleeper ideas are neglected.

How do you select the best information?

To be able to prioritise and select the collected knowledge, a designer needs a deep and broad understanding of the topic—clustering findings and organising them rationally. If the research is part of a group process with several people involved, it is also essential to find consensus on what exactly is the essence of any research. A clearly defined point of view is often needed to produce a well-defined goal.

A mind map can be an effective way to summarise and visualise the conclusions of the research process. A clear mind map is a combination of exacting keywords and clear visuals, in themed clusters and with linked information. It's a graphic layout of ideation that makes use of colour-coding to differentiate the various information clusters.

The attitude needed to select findings

• Role models: the judge, and the jury
• Mindset: critical and independent

Facts and findings...but a good brief also needs ambition.

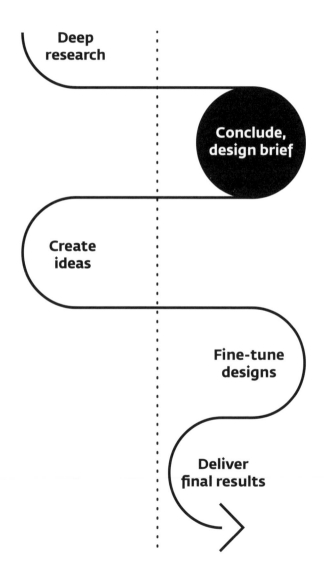

Deep research

Conclude, design brief

Create ideas

Fine-tune designs

Deliver final results

3 • Write a design brief

What is a design brief?

An inspirational design brief is a written summarisation of the most important findings of the research process, a clear definition of the design problem, and a description of why it is relevant or even urgent.

How do you make a design brief?

A design brief is a document that clearly defines what the problem is and why it needs to be solved. But it is not just that. It should demonstrate ambition and imagination. It should define possible directions or desired outcomes with target groups and stakeholders in mind. And it should all be done with empathy, not just academic logic. Design briefs can be made with clients or for clients. Or they can be the result of self-initiated research not commissioned by any clients at all.

What attitude is needed to write a design brief?

• Role models: writers and notaries
• Mindset: imaginative and accurate

Ideas are the rocket fuel for all design.

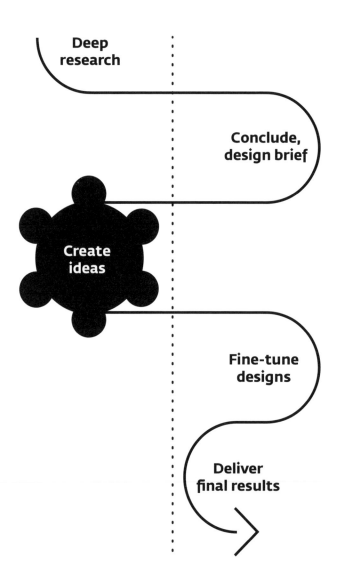

Deep research

Conclude, design brief

Create ideas

Fine-tune designs

Deliver final results

4 • Create ideas

What is creating ideas?

Creating ideas is also called creativity or ideation. It means coming up with smart solutions—constructs of the mind—for given problems. Ideas can have four qualities: originality, relevance, value, and urgency. Originality means that ideas have to have an aspect of newness. Relevance means they have to solve in an adequate way problems found during research and defined in the design brief. As mentioned before, value can be economic, social, and ecological value. Imaginative ideas can be exciting and original, but if they are not valuable or relevant, they are less effective. Ideas become urgent if they come at the right time and place, and solve a problem for a vital need or situation.

• *Precious Plastic. Plastic recycling project. Founder, Dave Hakkens. Founded: 2013.*

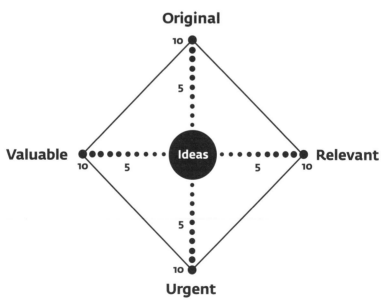

• Precious Plastic is a digital commons project, meaning that all the information produced by this open-source plastic recycling project, such as codes, drawings, and source materials, are available for free online. It ticks all the boxes: original, relevant, valuable, and urgent!

Think as freely as an artist!

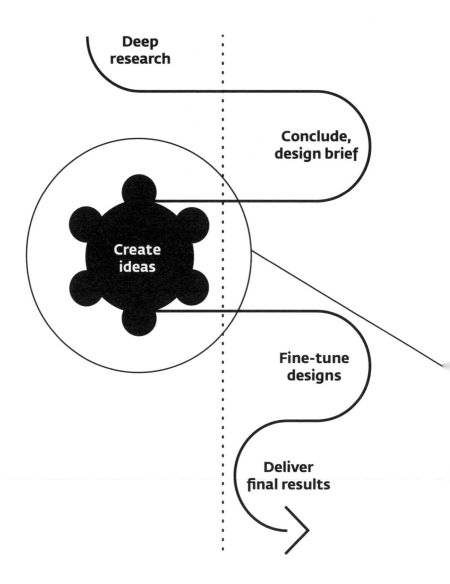

Deep research

Conclude, design brief

Create ideas

Fine-tune designs

Deliver final results

How do you create ideas?

The process of making ideas divides into two distinct and isolated steps. Step one is to create ideas with a mindset of complete freedom. It is crucial there be no limitations. Only after creating ideas does step two of the process start: selecting, judging, and adjusting. This second step— iteration—is the process of fine-tuning ideas and will be discussed in the next section, number 5. The two steps should never be merged or happen simultaneously.

During the first step—ideation—the necessary mindset is to have no judgment. Children are very good at this; they do not feel embarrassment or shame in their actions and in expressing themselves. This is exactly the mindset needed: instantly visualising a flow of different ideas!

Mistakes are an integrated part of creating ideas. Without mistakes, there is no exploration and experimentation. Both are needed to find the boundary between what might work and what is too extreme or no longer effective. Only by going too far can you ultimately define what the optimised idea is.

What is the right attitude to create ideas?
• Role models: artists and creatives
• Mindset: complete freedom and no judgment

The second part of this publication (starting on page 60) is about practical methods to create ideas. They can be learned and internalised by regular and repetitive use and can boost creativity.

A perfectionist's precision and skill are needed to fine-tune ideas.

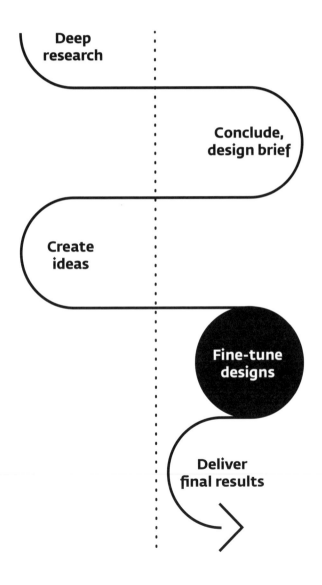

Deep research

Conclude, design brief

Create ideas

Fine-tune designs

Deliver final results

5 · Select & fine-tune ideas

What is selecting and fine-tuning ideas?

After making ideas in complete freedom, designers need to evaluate the different ideas to see if they are suitable. This part of the design process is called iteration. Some ideas will appear excellent and useful, others will not (or at least not yet), and will need further optimising and fine-tuning. Ideally, your ideas will score high on all four aspects of being original, relevant, valuable, and urgent.

How do you select and fine-tune ideas?

Fine-tuning ideas means making iterations to see if changing details make the selected ideas better. It can be alterations in shape or meaning or in making combinations to test for improvement. When fine-tuning, it is crucial always to make ideas visual and to preserve the previous steps so that you may compare steps against one another and judge the progress.

Consulting others, like colleagues or people representing your target groups, can speed up the fine-tuning process and provide a fresh perspective on your progress.

What attitude is needed?
• Role model: a craftsperson
• Mindset: empathic and perfectionistic

Process control is as vital as good design.

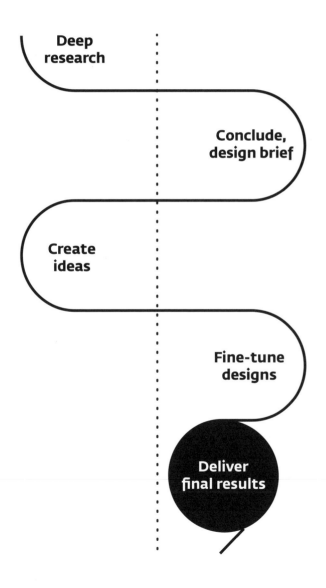

Deep
research

Conclude,
design brief

Create
ideas

Fine-tune
designs

Deliver
final results

6 • Deliver results

What is delivery?
Timing is an integral part of the design process. Having a great design solution but delivering too late can make the result useless. Planning and timing are as equally important as coming up with a spot-on design solution.

How do you deliver?
Time management is an integral part of the process of any design project. Dividing the project into clearly defined steps and moments to evaluate whether everything is going according to plan or not is essential. Sometimes designers do this themselves, and sometimes project managers are involved in making it happen. Another part of project management and being able to deliver the right solution at the right time is working on clear and open communication between team members, commissioners, and others involved.

What is the necessary attitude?
• Role model: a project manager
• Mindset: in control

It does not matter if the logic comes after the look. If an idea works, it works.

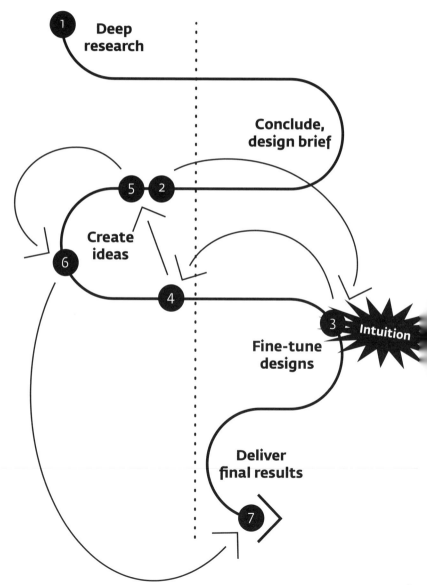

1 Deep research

Conclude, design brief

5 2

Create ideas

6

4

3 Intuition

Fine-tune designs

Deliver final results

7

Reversed ideating

There is no wrong order, only a wrong result

The second half of the design process, the part of making ideas and fine-tuning design does not always have to follow orderly logic. An idea can start with a visual shape, an inspirational cue, a gut feeling, or an intuition. Or it can initiate with something that is considered beautiful, though it is unclear how exactly it connects to the given design problem or brief. In cases like this, when the aesthetic precedes the meaning, people often conclude it is of no use and, therefore, that it should not be taken any further. But this is not always true! If a logical connection with the formulated design brief appears at a later stage, it can become a good or even excellent design solution. Of course, it still needs visualisation, designing, and fine-tuning (all the other steps of the process), but in the end, no one cares which came first: the shape, or the idea.

Reversed ideating might be in contradiction to the structure and stages of the design process, but creativity and exploring new paths do not always follow logic or reason. Logic and reason can appear and be put to use later during the process. That is important to keep in mind when creating and exploring freely and out of sequence. Once you become familiar with the sequence, you can apply your knowledge of the design process and complete the missing steps.

Again, it does not matter in what order an idea came to life. As long as it is original, has value, and it solves the design problem, no one cares if the logic came after the look. If it works, it works.

Part 2

Right Brain

- How to create visual ideas
- Imagination, creativity, and innovation
- Six methods to create ideas
- Idea-creation summarised

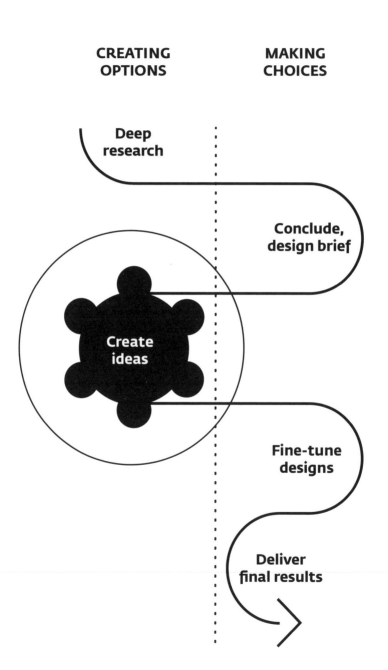

CREATING
OPTIONS

MAKING
CHOICES

Deep
research

Conclude,
design brief

Create
ideas

Fine-tune
designs

Deliver
final results

Ideating
Constructing
Crafting
Researching
Opinionating
Combining
Adventuring
Failing
Destructing
Organising
Dreaming
Visualising
Testing
Analysing
Editing
Imagining
+ - x :   Optimising
_____

Idea-driven design

Good ideas will always be needed and are powerful if they are original, relevant, valuable, and urgent.

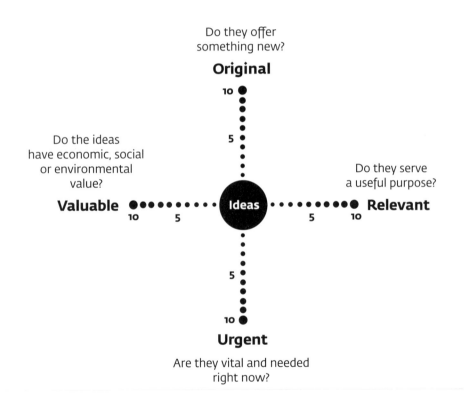

Do they offer
something new?

Original

Do the ideas
have economic, social
or environmental
value?

Do they serve
a useful purpose?

Valuable 10 5 **Ideas** 5 10 **Relevant**

Urgent

Are they vital and needed
right now?

How to create visual ideas

Ideas are the future

Ideas and creativity are the future. We need good ideas in many different
situations to solve design problems, and more. The second part of this
book covers different ways to create more and better ideas—how to
employ powerful techniques that boost creativity. It is about finding the
practical skills to come up with original, relevant, and valuable ideas—
skills that can be learned and developed. Such skills are very useful for all
types of designers, but also lead to methods that are effective in creating
ideas that can go beyond the context of design.

Ingredients of good ideas

As mentioned before, generally, good ideas have four qualities: originality, relevance, value, and urgency. Originality means that the ideas are
something we have not seen before. Relevance means they adequately
solve the defined problems. Value can be economical, but also social and
ecological. And finally, ideas are urgent if they come at the right time
and place to solve a vital problem.

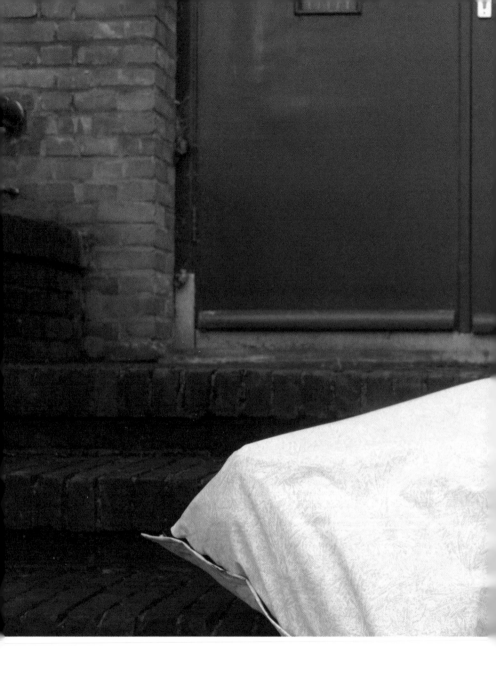

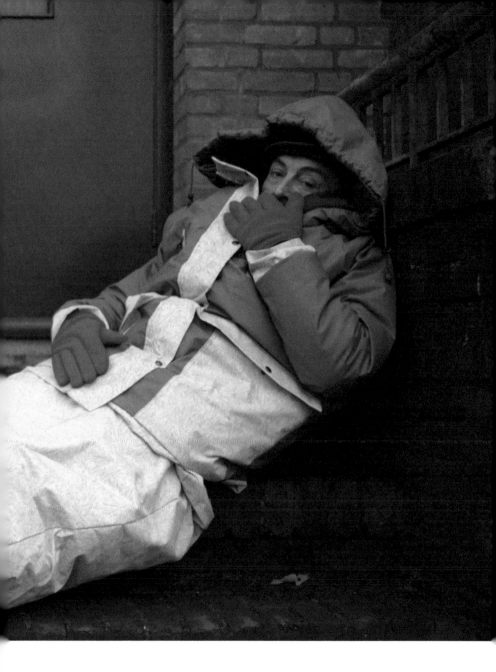

A Sheltersuit coat can easily transform into a sleeping bag for full-body protection.

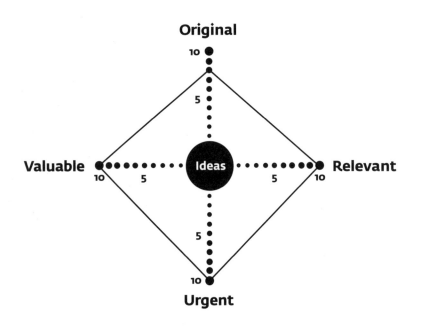

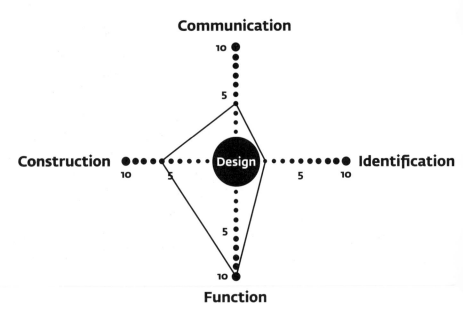

• Sheltersuit. Founder, Bas Timmer. 2014.

The Sheltersuit is a waterproof and windproof outfit that provides full-body protection. It is made of recycled and up-cycled materials. Suits are given away for free to homeless people and refugees around the world. Many Sheltersuit employees were once refugees themselves. They know from personal experience what it is like to have to live outdoors.

Creating ideas requires practice and exercise.

Generating multiple ideas is better because they provide different angles and therefore more possibilities.

Creativity is a talent, but it is also something you can learn and develop.

Train your brain

Creating ideas means finding different perspectives—recognising diverse ways of seeing. This can be learned by using the methods offered in this second part of the book, and by continuously using those ways of thinking to train your brain as you would strengthen a muscle. Some of these methods might immediately feel familiar, while others might not. Some might even feel very uncomfortable at first. But by making regular use of all the different ways of creating ideas, you will gradually come to find them second nature. You will develop the ability to internalise them and be able to switch between them to make more and better ideas faster.

Why is more better?

Generating more ideas is beneficial because it becomes more likely that you will see a problem from many different angles. It offers the possibility to choose afterwards which of those angels is the better one. Committing to the first idea that comes to mind might feel good. But if that first idea happens to be the wrong one later in the process, there is no fall-back plan, or alternative except to start from scratch again.

Born creative

Creativity is not just for those who we consider to be born creative, or who are in creative professions. Of course, it helps if you have some sort of natural talent, but it is vital to realise that you can learn creativity and create valuable ideas by regularly exercising your mind.

Imagination is the ability to come up with ideas not first experienced with our senses.

Original ideas with value and relevance are the ideas we consider creative.

Innovation is the process of creating ideas that transform organisations or systems.

Imagination, creativity, and innovation

Is there a difference?

Some say they are more or less the same: imagination, creativity, and innovation. But there are some important distinctions among them.

Imagination

Imagination is coming up with ideas not first experienced with our senses: things we don't see, hear, feel, smell, or taste. Ideas are produced in our mind first and then can be expressed or executed back into the physical world.

Creativity

Creativity is the ability to come up with original ideas that have value and that are relevant. 'Original' means that an idea has the quality of being new. As mentioned before, value can be economic, social, or ecological. Imaginative ideas can be exciting and original, but if they only have those qualities, then they lack value. Ideas become 'relevant' or even urgent if they appear at the right time and place.

Innovation

Innovation is the process of bringing creative ideas into practice, implementing them and making them useful. Creativity is part of the innovation process, but the execution involves more and different people and organisations to interact and transform systems.

Modern art is an excellent inspiration for new ideas.

Ideas made visual are tested ideas and can be shared.

Inspiration in art

Modern and contemporary art can be an excellent inspiration for new ideas, sometimes even more so than other design. Like design, they often use visual means, but they generally have more freedom to express and explore. Going to museums and seeing art exhibitions can be a great way to find new ways of thinking.

Make ideas visual

As mentioned, while creating ideas, it is essential to make them visible instantly for two reasons:

• First, because it is the best way to test if what you are thinking works or doesn't.

• The second reason is to be able to communicate and explain the ideas to a team with whom you collaborate, or to a client. Visualising is testing—a reality check—seeing what is good about it or what can be improved. Making it visual is instant communication.

The mindset of a scrapyard worker.

1 • Deconstruct - Reconstruct
Break it, re-make it

This method of creating ideas is about taking things apart, discovering all the details to understand the big picture: analysing, leaving parts out, editing. Take time to focus on only a few small details, and then rebuild something with a new meaning or message. 'Deconstruct - Reconstruct' can turn out to be just recycling, but it can also prove to be a lot more.

• Onderlangs. Idea and execution, Paul Bogaers. 2007.

Onderlangs is a novel by photographer and artist Paul Bogaers that he constructed by borrowing complete sentences chosen form 250 existing books, all manually rearranged to compose a surprising and tantalising new story. It took him fifteen years to finish the book.

• *Millegomme. Part of Refunc. Founders, Jan Körbes & Denis Oudendijk. 2005. Millegomme means 'one thousand tires' in Italian. It is a project by garbage and recyclables architects Jan Körbes and Denis Oudendijk in which they created objects, toys, furniture, and architecture out of used car tires.*

Guard

45p
Monday
November 7
1988
Published in London
and Manchester

Tory right pushes for radicalism

Hurd aide quits to speak his mind

Stephen Bates
Political Correspondent

J

ONE, Mark's latest ....

That governments can simply fall back and consolidate past achievements is not the case.

Slate comes out for private finance, page 11

• *The Guardian edited. © Marc Shillum. 1996.*
By only removing words and images from given pages of the newspaper, new con-
nections and meanings come to the surface—a smart example of deconstruction.

The mindset of a magnet.

2 • Forced fit
Connect the unconnected

Forced fit means making surprising, unconventional combinations, like when sampled music connects an unlikely pairing of sounds. The association of unexpected elements only works when it is wonderfully clever—when something 'clicks' in the partnership.

Powerful combinations

Many projects start with a given place, object, set of keywords, or tailored message. Associating the given with something unlikely and unexpected can lead to surprisingly useful results. If you look around, you will find many design solutions based on a forced fit idea.

McLips

Imagine: a typical glossy ad for red lipstick. The brand is Chanel. The red is bright, and the holder is shiny black and gold. But instead of having the double C initials embossed on the top, the McDonalds 'double arches' is visible. The tag line says, 'McLips—Strawberry forever'. The clever match: both products have a connection with the human mouth. The tension that makes this image memorable is the odd mix of luxury with fast food.

• *Dust furniture. Studio Makkink & Bey. 2004.*

Air is what makes the connection between the vacuum cleaner and the inflatable chair. That's the clever match. After using the vacuum cleaner, you can comfortably sit on the inflatable chair filled with the dust collected.

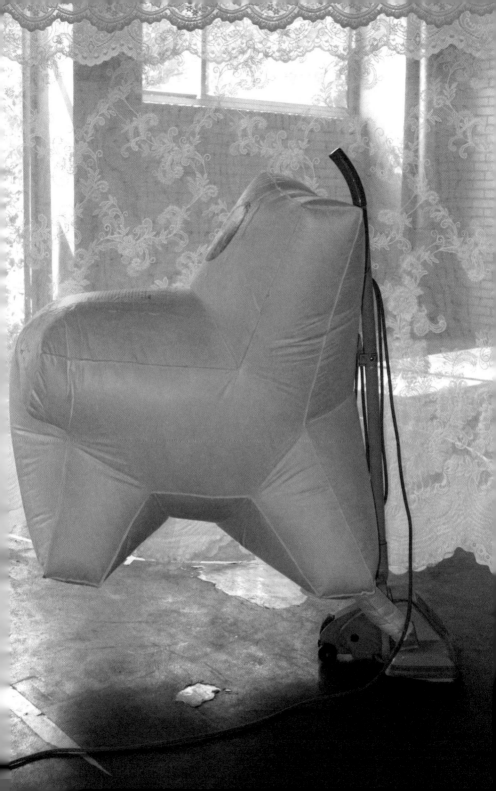

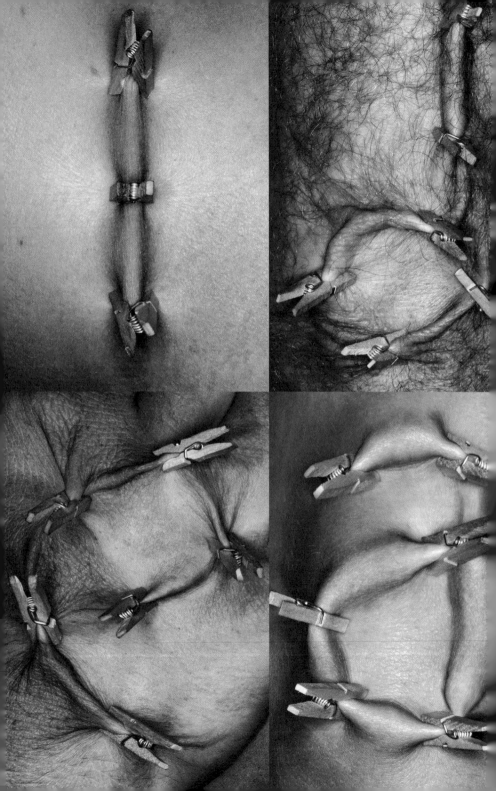

• *Typeface in Skin. Idea and design, Thijs Verbeek. Photography, Arjan Benning. 2006-2008.*
An alphabet created with clothespins and skin. The clothespins are more than just a tool to keep the folds in place. The fact that both textile and human skin can fold is the clever match.

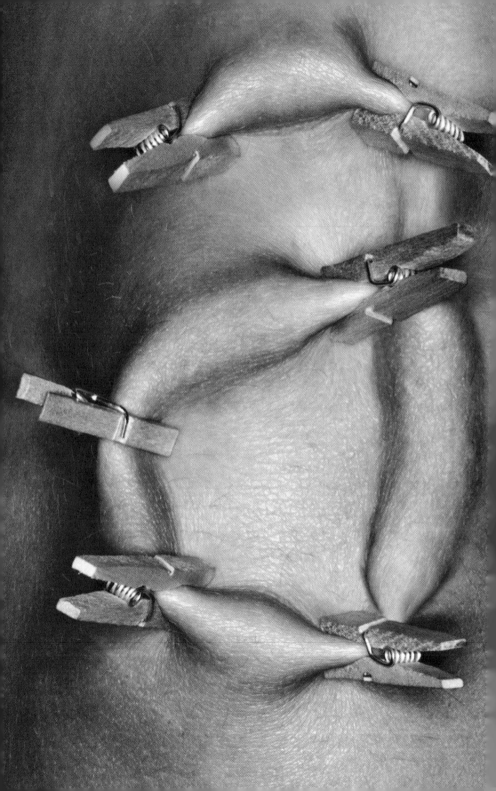

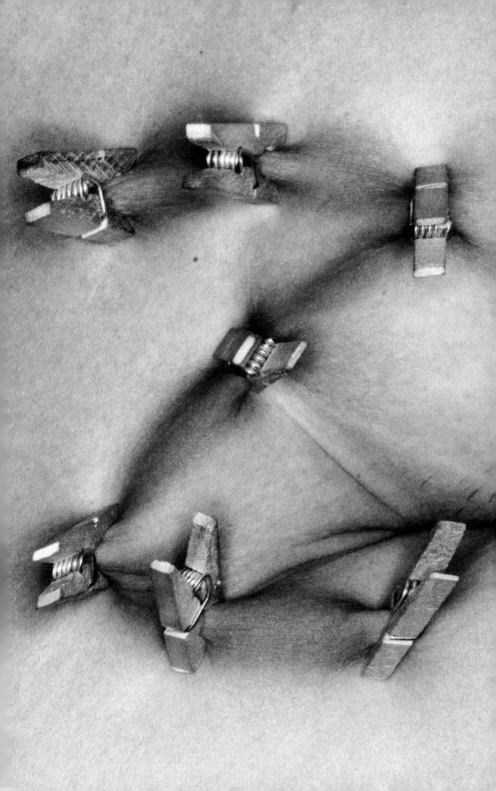

• Refunc. Founders, Jan Körbes & Denis Oudendijk. Founded 2003.
Refunc reconnects people and material by changing people's perception of functionality and making them aware of the value of existing materials. This hybrid of a bicycle and a garbage container 'clicks' because both have wheels. Most forced fit ideas need this clever match, a detail that makes parts connect.

The mindset of a mental chameleon.

3 • Empathise
Think as different professionals

An effective and empathic way to come up with ideas is to imagine you are someone in a different profession. Imagine the solutions such another person would come up with looking at the given design problem. Throughout the process you can switch between different professions, imagining the perspective of each and the way they come to their own solutions.

Get into the minds of others

How does a mathematician approach a problem? Or a writer, politician, philosopher, visual artist, dancer, astronaut, musician, clown, alien, scientists, journalist, chef, chauffeur, programmer, architect, pilot, biologist, sailor, geologist. By empathising with multiple perspectives, you will discover equally varied outcomes.

Think as different people in different professions.

Think as a
Mathematician
Writer
Politician
Philosopher
Visual artist
Dancer
Space traveller
Musician
Clown
Martian
Scientists
Chef
Journalist
Chauffeur
Programmer
Architect
Pilot
Biologist
Sailor
Shopkeeper

The mindset of Madonna and Ali G in one body.

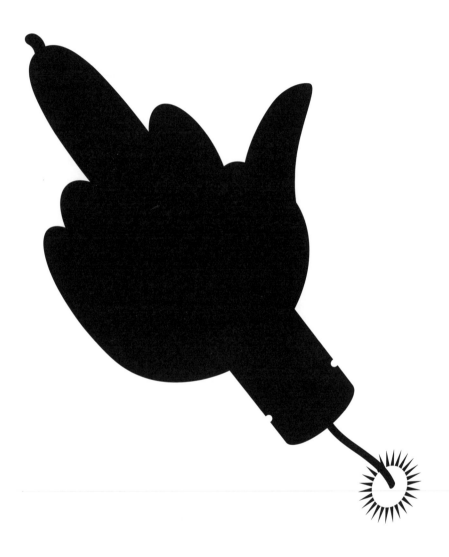

4 • Provocation
Go for the shock effect

Making ideas memorable is an outstanding ability. Being provocative is how to make that happen. To be provocative is to look for surprises and extremes—for bold, spectacular ideas that push expectations and that are on, or over, the edge. It can be achieved by deliberately going too far and exaggerating to find out where exactly that edge is. If you are not willing to go too far, it becomes hard to find provocative ideas. Remember, you can always take a step back from the edge later, if needed.

Tattooed pigs

An outstanding example of provocation is a project by the Belgian visual artist Wim Delvoye named Tattooed Pigs. He decorated the skins of different pigs with the typical symbols and messages that we usually find on the human skin.

Portrait of pope

The portrait of former Pope Benedict XVI by the US artist Niki Johnson is another example of a provocative work. It is called Eggs Benedict and made with 17,000 colourful condoms organised on an invisible metal grid. It is a visual protest against the conservative attitude towards birth control by this pope, and the Catholic church in general, in relation to the prevention of HIV/AIDS.

• *Viktor & Rolf upside-down shop, Milan. Design, Siebe Tettero, with Sherrie Zwail at SZI Design, Amsterdam, and CLS Architetti, Milan. 2005.*
It is a luxury fashion store interior fantastically mixing classical architectural styles. The provocation is executed at the highest possible level: one detail, the orientation of the whole interior, is turned upside-down. You find yourself walking on the ceiling.

• Smoke. Maarten Baas. Photography, Maarten van Houten. 2002.
The Smoke Rietveld REDBLUE chair and the Smoke ZIGZAG chair are design icons
that have been set afire in a controlled way. The surface is protected with a clear
epoxy resin after the burn, keeping them from degrading further. Normally burning
means destroying. In this case, every chair is given a unique personality.

The mindset of your little cousin.

5 • Act! Act! Act!
First do, then think

If logic and reason no longer work, taking action is the best way to create ideas. Jumping into action is liberating because it means doing without thinking—just going by intuition and with complete freedom. It needs a mindset whereby you choose to let go of embarrassment and shame.

Know and flow

Just simply taking action can be very useful, especially right after you first absorb all relevant knowledge about the problem. If you then do something entirely disassociated (like going for a run or sleeping), you can begin making visuals with an empty mindset. Let ideas flow—with no judgment at all. Visualise whatever comes to mind. Let go of analysing and selecting at this stage. That you do later.

Childlike freedom

To enter the right mindset, it can be helpful to look at how children work and play. They are very good at free thinking. They initiate work and play without hesitation, and are happy to come up with a story or a rationale after an activity is completed.

Draw with eyes closed

A useful exercise in visualising without too much embarrassment or self-awareness is to make images with your eyes closed, without looking while doing. The outcome will have a free and uncontrolled quality. That spirit and freedom is something to try to maintain going further, making visuals.

• *Free drawings by Kas, five years old. 2019.*

The mindset of a fish on a mountain.

6 • Counter context
Change place, change time

How we understand and interpret situations and give meaning to visuals and messages is culturally defined. Any situation will be read differently in different cultures in the world. Time also affects how we understand (visual) messages. What was commonly accepted a century ago will be perceived differently today. Being aware of and understanding cultural conventions opens you up to the possibility of making changes and creating exciting ideas.

Change place

Meaning is often related to place. Environment defines how you understand a situation, location, or object. By simply changing environment, you will understand the meaning or message in a new way, and the idea can become more memorable:
• A dinosaur walking on the moon
• A crystal chandelier hanging over a road to provide streetlight

Change time

Changing context also applies to time. Changing time can introduce new meaning:
• The Cannes film festival curated by Vincent van Gogh
• Mona Lisa with no wifi connection on her smartphone

Fountain

A famous example of changing place from art history is Fountain, a work by Dadaist, Marcel Duchamp, made in 1917. By placing a urinal in a typical museum setting, he challenged the perception of a sculptural work of art. Changing the place changed the object's meaning.

• Sandbox, Amsterdam. Idea and execution, Harmen de Hoop. 1996.
Paving stones were removed, and sand and toys were added to create a playground for children.

Create more, diverse ideas!

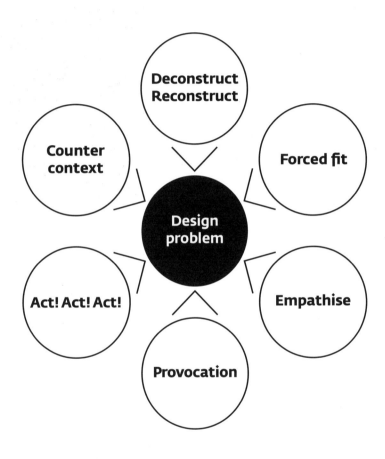

Idea creation summarised

Learn to swap between methods

You can learn each and every of these methods to create visual ideas, and all of them can be equally useful. It takes steady practice to make all the different methods a part of one's repertoire. The best way is to start working with just one method, then add another, and then another. After some time, it will be possible to shift among them. Doing so will make your output more diverse and the ideas faster, easier, better, and more plentiful.

Know what is needed, what you are good at, and when to involve other experts.

Know what is needed. Know your strength

Some creatives or designers specialise in the first part of the design process and focus only on research. Others are good at creating ideas and concepts. Still, another may decide to become a very good craftsperson, concentrating on executing ideas.

No one has to be a specialist in each and every aspect. True, a good understanding of all steps is necessary to deliver optimised solutions—to be able to develop the best ideas and design solutions. But for the aspects that you are not good at, it is essential to recognise those shortcomings and team with specialists in the design process.

A world of experience in design and an ocean of passion for education.

Afterword

About the bookmaker

Joost Roozekrans has been working for over thirty years as a designer, creative director, and design educator. He trained as a visual communication designer in the Netherlands and worked in The Hague, London, and Shanghai.

Joost has given design lectures and workshops around the world, as he has a passion for education. This publication is a comprehensive reflection of his personal experience and the things he has learned in the world of design. He has an eclectic taste of music, loves Asian cuisine, and visiting megacities and museums. He has a motto: 'If you look very, very closely, everything becomes interesting.'

Thank you!

Respect

My fellow travelers
Many people helped me to explore my ideas, encouraged me, gave me confidence. They helped me understand more about life and grow in my profession. I want to thank all of them!

In more or less chronological order, special thank-yous go to
Kees Roozekrans, Ludo Koks, Frie van der Heijden, Ton van Nijnatten,
Jan van Mechelen, Toon Stalpers, Frans Jaspers, Hartmut Kowalke,
Henk Cornelissen, Sjoerd de Vries, Gert Dumbar, Kitty de Jong,
Michel de Boer, Liza Enebeis, Marc Shillum, Simon Esterson,
Carolyn Finlayson, Lonneke Jansma, Bob van Dijk, Bas Leurs,
Oscar Smeulders, Louise de Blécourt, Henk Willems, Elizabeth Pick,
Zhengfang Zou, Shi Ming, Lin Rong, Daan Roggeveen, Karmen Kekic,
Wang Min, Chen Ziye, Li Tianjiao, all my Shanghai students,
Rene Toneman, Dennis Flinterman, Jorn Dal, and Marijke Meester.

Contributions
This publication has been made possible with the support of the Design Management Network.

Pictures of projects were kindly provided by various artists and designers. I want to thank them for their inspirational works and their generosity.

Fedra Sans font family
This publication is type-set in the Latin version of Fedra Sans, an international multi-lingual font family supporting most of the world's languages, and developed by type foundry Typotheque (www.typoteque.com).

Bring a message or tell a story.
(Advertising & Communication Design)

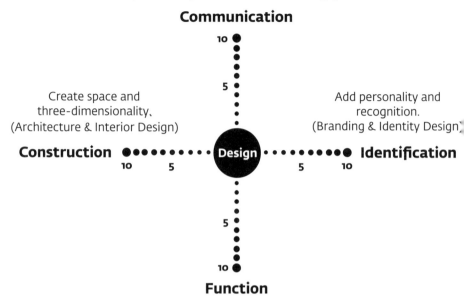

Communication

Create space and
three-dimensionality.
(Architecture & Interior Design)

Add personality and
recognition.
(Branding & Identity Design)

Construction ●●●●●●●●● **Design** ●●●●●●●●● **Identification**

10   5   5   10

Function

Improve usability and navigation.
(Product & Interface Design)

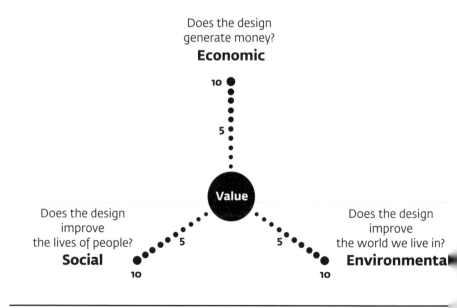

Does the design
generate money?

Economic

Does the design
improve
the lives of people?

Does the design
improve
the world we live in?

Social

Value

Environmental

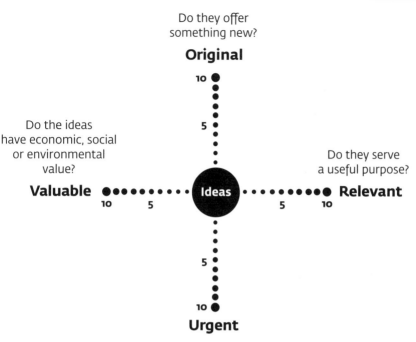

Do they offer
something new?

Original

10
5

Do the ideas
have economic, social
or environmental
value?

Do they serve
a useful purpose?

Valuable ● ● ● ● ● ● ● ● ● ● **Ideas** ● ● ● ● ● ● ● ● ● ● **Relevant**
10   5   5   10

5

10

Urgent

Are they vital and needed
right now?

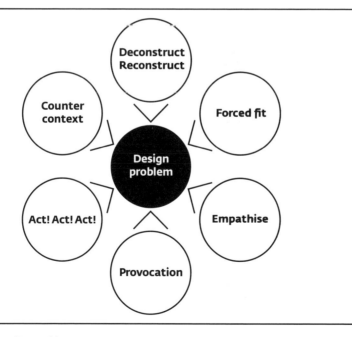

Deconstruct
Reconstruct

Counter
context

Forced fit

Design
problem

Act! Act! Act!

Empathise

Provocation

DESIGN PROCESS • The snake

Create options	Make choices	**What?**
Deep research		• Build an in-depth understanding of topic or problem that needs solving
	Conclude, design brief	• Select findings • Prioritise • Draw conclusions • Write design brief
Create ideas		• Create ideas that are original, relevant, valuable, and urgent
	Fine-tune designs	• Evaluate ideas • Fine tune and optimise • Define shape and design
	Deliver final results	• Process control • Manage time • Manage expectations

How?	Role model
• Use only sources with authority • Verify all key findings • Does the source have an interest?	• Journalist and scientist • Mindset: eager and curious
• Organise findings with logic • Define point of view • Include target groups • Make mind map	• Judge and jury • Mindset: critical and independent
• Deconstruct - Reconstruct • Forced fit • Empathise • Provocation • Act! Act! Act! • Counter context	• Artist and creative • Mindset: freedom and no judgment
• Make iterations or combinations • Improve details • Ask colleagues or target groups for feedback	• Craftsperson • Mindset: empathic and perfectionist
• Define clear steps • Define responsibilities • Evaluate and communicate	• Project manager • Mindset: in control

'Insightful and resourceful.
Great practical tools to create design
ideas.' – Wang Min.

'Roozekrans tells a very clear story
about design as an engine for
innovation: how you do it, stimulate
it, evaluate it and improve it. Read!'–
Toon Lauwen.

Cover recommendations

Wang Min

Professor Wang Min was Dean of the School of Design at China Central Academy of Fine Arts (CAFA), the most prestigious art school in China, and Design Director of the 2008 Beijing Olympics. Having held many other positions, he notably was the Vice President of ICOGRADA, the International Council of Graphic Design Associations, and Senior Art Director at AdobeSystems. Currently, he is the co-chair of a BA and MA design program and a design studio in Shanghai, together with Michel de Boer.

Toon Lauwen

Writer and curator Toon Lauwen has written and co-produced 14 books on design and architecture for international publishers and published three under his own WOTH; ways of thinking label. He is the publisher of WOTH Wonderful Things Magazine and producer and consultant in design, strategy & communication. As a curator, he exported design exhibitions to the USA, Australia, New Zealand, and several European museums and venues.

BIS Publishers
Building Het Sieraad
Postjesweg 1
1057 DT Amsterdam
The Netherlands
T +31 (0)20 515 02 30
bis@bispublishers.com
www.bispublishers.com

ISBN 978 90 6369 586 6

Copyright © 2020 Joost Roozekrans & BIS Publishers
www.joostroozekrans.com

Colophon

Author: Joost Roozekrans
Design & artwork: Joost Roozekrans
Text advice: Chen Ziye
Copy edit: John Loughlin
Typeface: Fedra Sans – Typotheque

Images are generously provided by
Studio Dumbar, pages 12-13
Precious Plastic, pages 17, 49-51
Sheltersuit – Bas Timmer, pages 66-67, 69
Paul Bogaers, pages 78-79
Millegomme – Jan Körbes, Denis Oudendijk, page 80-81
Marc Shillum, pages 82-83
Studio Makkink & Bey, page 87
Thijs Verbeek, pages 88, 90-91
Refunc – Jan Körbes, Denis Oudendijk, page 93
Siebe Tettero, page 100
Maarten Baas, pages 102-103
Kas Roozekrans, pages 106-107
Harmen de Hoop, pages 110-111

*If you look very, very closely,
everything becomes interesting.*